Paddy Brosnan is a mindfulness & meditation teacher, inspirational speaker, and author.

In his early thirties, Paddy experienced a radical shift in how he wanted to live his life. This marked the beginning of an intense inward journey of spiritual development. He left the world of business and devoted the next several years to developing his awareness through the practice of mindfulness and meditation. In the years since, he has devoted himself to understanding and deepening this transformation.

Paddy's teachings are simple but at the same time profound. At the heart of this is a very direct and accessible insight into how the development of awareness can ultimately bring us a deeper sense of contentment and happiness. This simple message, delivered with humour and compassion, has helped countless people find inner peace and fulfilment in their lives.

Paddy is a sought-after public speaker and travels extensively, delivering workshops and retreats as well as visiting schools to encourage mindfulness in children.

Paddy's first book, *This Works: How to Use Mindfulness to Calm the Hell Down and Just Be Happy*, was published by Hay House in 2018. www.paddybrosnan.com

Praise for *This Works*

"Paddy Brosnan has a gift for making mindfulness and the philosophy behind it immediately understandable in everyday life."

Padraig O'Morain

"Great book. I like the simplicity with which Paddy describes engaging in this process. If you are new to mindfulness or looking for a new perspective, then this book is a great investment. I highly recommend it."

Colin White

"Really love the way Paddy talks to you and not at you."

Stephen Caldwell

"Amazing and inspiring, everybody needs this."

Pauline Mooney

"So insightful and encouraging to know we can achieve a better quality of life through the practice of mindful living and daily meditation. "

Karen Nic Mhathúna

Treasury of Mindfulness

Paddy Brosnan

Dalzell Press

First published in 2020 by Dalzell Press.

Dalzell Press
54 Abbey Street
Bangor, N. Ireland
BT20 4JB

ISBN 978-0-9563864-8-9

The information provided in this book should not be treated as a substitute for professional medical advice; always consult a medical practitioner. Any use of the information and mindfulness exercises in this book is at the sole discretion and risk of the reader. Neither the author or the publisher can be held responsible for any loss, claim or damage arising out of the use, or misuse, of the information and exercises in this book, the failure to take medical advice, or for any material on Paddy Brosnan's website or any third-party websites cited in this book

To Rosie,

Wherever you are,

I hope you're finding joy.

"Living mindfully, living with awareness,
is the only way to ensure that you miss none of
your life, and that you at least have the
opportunity to experience all of it."

—Paddy Brosnan

Mindfulness

Is…

Moment by moment awareness of your thoughts, feelings, and environment.

Is…

Moment by moment awareness and acceptance of your thoughts, feelings, and environment.

Is…

Moment by moment awareness and acceptance of your thoughts, feelings, and environment without judgement.

Is…

Moment by moment awareness and acceptance of your thoughts, feelings, and environment without judgement and without an anxious need for them to be different.

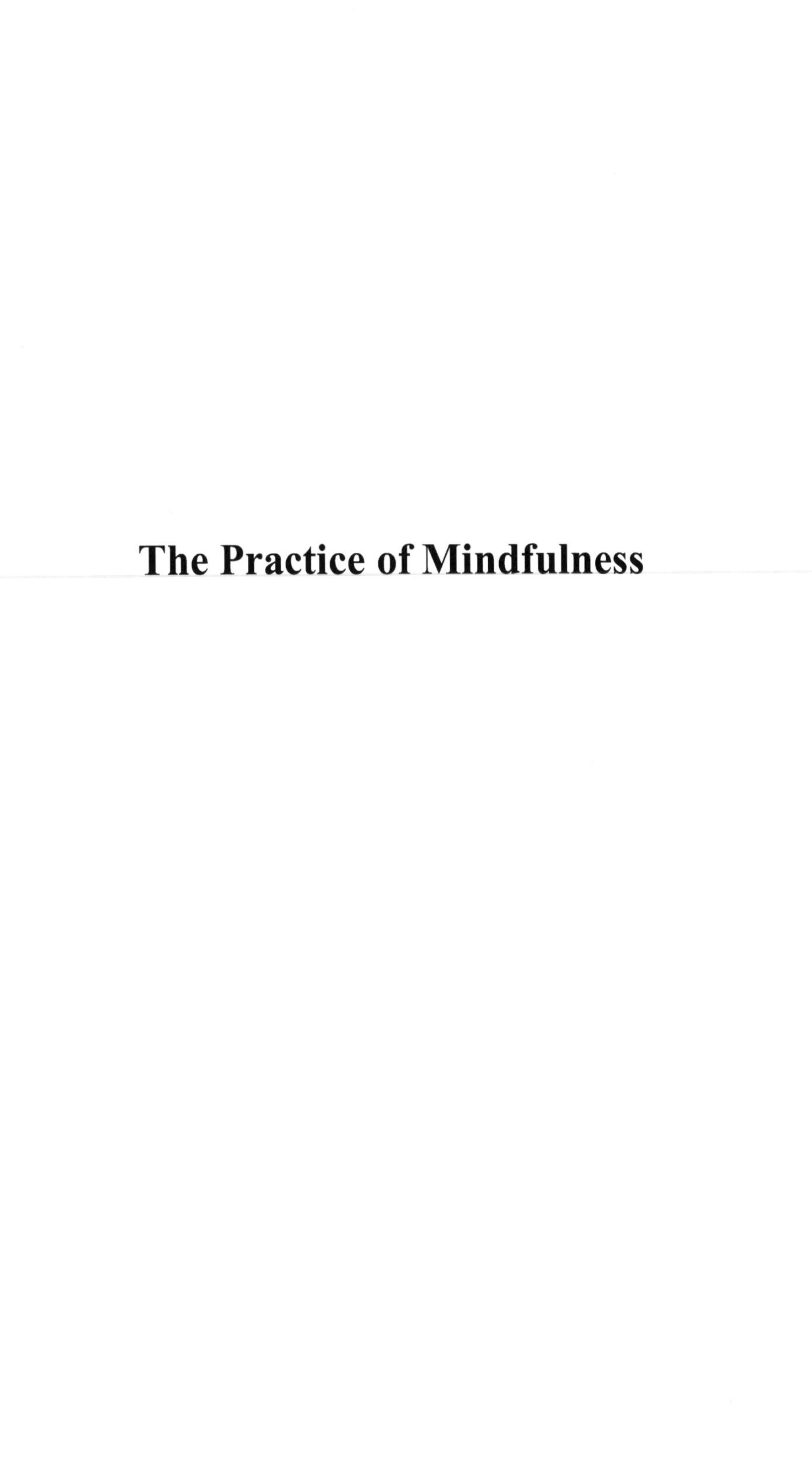

The Practice of Mindfulness

I started practicing mindfulness fifteen years ago. Back then, the way mindfulness was taught was fairly simple and straightforward. Over the years, I have witnessed this beautiful and simple practice become ever more complicated.

Mindfulness has been taken to mean "a specific technique to deal with or treat a specific problem," like the use of mindful meditation to treat stress or anxiety. However effective this may be, it is an application of mindfulness, an aspect of mindfulness. Carrots may be a part of your dinner, but it would be wrong to call your entire meal carrots when in fact it's a Sunday roast.

I suggest that it is more accurate to view mindfulness as a way of seeing the world, your world, rather than as a technique to be applied to certain parts of it.

Mindfulness is a way of being, of living your life,

it is not another chore to add to your list of things to do.

We Practice Mindfulness in Order to Live Mindfully

In this little Treasury, I hope you find inspiration and guidance to adopt and develop the simple practice of mindfulness. In doing so, you will find that with patience and dedication, you will be living a more mindful and aware life. I urge you to discover for yourself the difference that living mindfully will bring to your life and the lives of those you love.

—*Paddy Brosnan*

"You can live life in your mind or live life in your life. Mindfulness affords you the opportunity to choose."

—Paddy Brosnan

The Practice of Mindfulness

We practice mindfulness in order to live mindfully and to reap the rewards that living mindfully brings. This practice takes two forms:

Mindful Meditation

The reason we engage in mindful meditation is to gently retrain the mind to be aware, to be mindful of what is going on right now. For most of our waking day, our mind is off somewhere, separate from our bodies and from what we are doing. We may be washing the dishes, but our mind is away in the future, worrying about tomorrow or it's back in the past, raking over old grievances. Mindful meditation trains the mind to be with the body and involved with the activity we are engaged in right now. Formal mindful meditation only takes a few minutes a day but the benefits to our mental wellbeing are huge.

Bringing Awareness to Our Everyday Lives

By bringing awareness and mindfulness to our everyday activities, we are continuing the work we started in our meditation. You could say that our meditation is like studying the "theory," and engaging in our normal tasks with mindfulness is the "practical" work. When we go about our ordinary mundane tasks with the full attention of mindfulness, we find that they cease being merely chores we have to complete—they take on a whole new vibrancy. Bringing our body, mind, and environment together in this way ensures that we miss none of what life has to offer and that we truly experience all of our days to the fullest.

Developing awareness and practicing mindfulness is one of the simplest things to learn. It involves just the two steps outlined above. But, as with any new skill, practice is required. If you want to play the piano, for example, you have to practice playing the piano. After some time, you become proficient and it becomes second nature. The difference of course is that living mindfully will have a much more beneficial effect on your life and the lives of those you love because you will not just be mastering a new skill, you will be adopting a different approach to your life as a whole.

To keep going with our practice, we need determination, energy, and a belief in the end result. My hope is that you will find the inspiration for these in the coming pages.

The Benefits of Mindfulness

Thousands of academic papers have been published on mindfulness, and there is no shortage of scientific proof as to the value of this beautiful and simple way of living. Here are just a few of the many benefits those who practice mindfulness and live mindfully experience:

- Less stress
- Less anxiety and depression
- A greater sense of joy and general wellbeing
- Higher levels of energy
- Less likely to suffer chronic pain
- Enhanced mental health and functioning

- Less prone to addiction
- Increased self-confidence
- A greater sense of compassion for self and others
- Enhanced resilience (the ability to be able to bounce back from challenge or trauma), especially in children, and
- The list goes on.

I have experienced all of these benefits and more in my own practice. For me (and for many of my students), the most positive change has been the dramatic drop in levels of "reactiveness." Let me explain. Before I started practicing and living mindfully, my reactive mind was fully engaged. I would react with annoyance or even anger at the smallest things. Inevitably, this caused suffering to me and to those I love most. The greatest gift that mindfulness has given me—and millions of others—is the gift of *calm*. I can see the serenity in letting things be as they are. In this state of calm, I understand that wanting things to be different crushes any joy I might experience in my life at any given moment. I have the space to decide—am I going to react to my thoughts or feelings, or just let them float on by?

In this calm I get to experience a beautiful truth: life only happens in the present moment.

"Keep knocking and the joy inside will eventually open a window and look out to see who's there."
—*Rumi*

"If there was one thing you could do right now to improve your life, improve your mental wellbeing, and reduce your suffering—regardless of your situation—it would be to practice mindfulness."
—*Paddy Brosnan*

It Takes Three to Be Present

The mind can focus on only one thing at a time. So, if our mind is engaged with what we are doing at any given moment, it can't be off somewhere else, worrying or "catastrophising." Likewise, if we are being mindful, our mind isn't free to react automatically, Instead, we get to choose which of our thoughts or emotions are worth acting on and which ones we can happily let be. To test this idea for yourself, please ponder the following statement for a few minutes, and see if you agree:

"We are most at ease when our body, mind, and environment are one."

Let's examine this statement …

Can you come up with any occasions in your own life in which this was true? For instance, have you ever looked out over a view that struck you as beautiful—a glorious sunset or the vista from the side of a mountain as you looked out on the stunning valley below? At that moment, you weren't thinking of anything else or doing anything else. Your mind, body, and environment were together. You were immersed in the scene in front of you. Do you remember how you felt? Were you at ease?

If you have children, can you recall the first time you saw or held them? What about when you hear your favourite song or piece of music? Or when you're engaged in an interesting conversation with a friend? These moments are magical, because these are the moments when we are naturally mindful, when our minds are with our bodies and fully focused on whatever we are doing. We are not caught in the suffering of stress, anxiety, or anything else. We are at ease. It follows that if we had more occasions, more moments, when our mind, body, and environment were together, we would feel at ease more often. The great news is that's exactly what we do when we introduce mindful moments into our day and routinely practice our formal mindful meditations. We fill our day with ease!

People have a hard time letting go of their suffering. Out of a fear of the unknown, they prefer suffering that is familiar."

—Thich Nhat Hanh

"Every day, think as you wake up, today I am fortunate to be alive, I have a precious human life, I am not going to waste it. I am going to use all my energies to develop myself."
—His Holiness, The 14th Dalai Lama

How to Use This Book

When the suggestion of writing this *Treasury of Mindfulness* was first put to me, I fell in love with the idea; a concept formed in my mind immediately. I wanted this book to be a true treasury—the image I had was of someone opening a treasure chest and rummaging around to find what they are looking for.

That's my suggestion to you as to how to use this book. First, read the preamble chapters and then, rummage around in the rest of the book to find exactly what you're looking for. Or, even better, open to a page randomly whenever the mood takes you (hopefully daily) and trust that whatever you've landed on is something you should try. Whichever page you land on, it will contain one of four different mindfulness practices…

-  Mindful Meditation
- 

Everyday Mindfulness

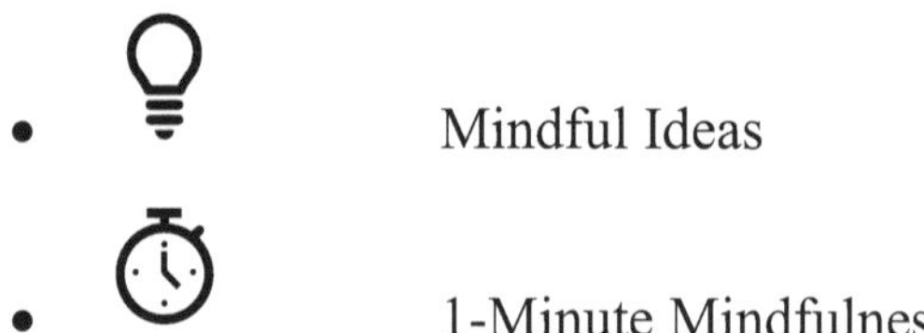

- Mindful Ideas
- 1-Minute Mindfulness

You'll find a description for each one below. I have also included a separate chapter that explains how to introduce mindfulness to kids and the benefits it will bring to their lives. Also included in that chapter are some fun mindful activities especially for children.

Scattered liberally throughout you will find beautiful quotes from inspirational people past and present—and some from me. A great way to use these is to think of them as your "thought for the day." Mull them over for a while before moving on.

Mindful Meditation

The practicalities of mindful meditation are simple. You need a room with a door you can close, so you are not disturbed, and you need a cushion or a chair to sit on. You do not need a completely quiet setting: normal family life can go on, just as long as you are not interrupted.

Ideally, you should practice formal mindful meditation for twenty minutes in the morning and evening. The morning session should be as soon as possible after you wake up and the evening session should be a few hours before you go to bed. It's important that you build up to twenty minutes gradually. If you have never meditated before or are just coming back to your practice, you might find that twenty minutes is too much. Try starting with five minutes for a week or so, then ten, and so on.

Sit on your chair or cushion with your back straight and your hands held lightly in your lap.

> Breathe in and out through your nose, and practice whichever one of the meditations takes your fancy. Once you have practiced this meditation for a few weeks (or for as long as it holds your interest), move on to another. If at any time during meditation you feel you are getting drowsy, open your eyes a little and "soft-focus" on nothing in particular about two or three feet in front of you.

Please do not concern yourself about whether you are doing it "right" or "wrong." Be gentle with yourself and try to avoid ALL self-criticism. You are gently retraining your mind, away from anxiety, stress, and suffering. Don't use your meditation time as another reason to beat yourself up. In the same way, don't have any expectations of your meditation practice. Try to see it as just meditating and nothing else—with no particular motive or goal. Adding these will just cause the very thing you are trying to alleviate, namely stress and suffering. Look on your meditation in the same way you might look on going for a walk—you're going nowhere in particular and for no special reason—you are just walking.

A word about excuses. Many people tell me that they couldn't possibly spare twenty minutes in the morning or evening. They then give me all the excuses they can to justify their claim. If you asked these same people if they would like to feel happier, be calmer, and (ultimately) to suffer less, they would almost certainly say YES! They (or you or I) can't have it both ways. The fact is that if they wanted to, they could find 20 minutes in the morning and evening! Evidence of the benefits of mindfulness has filled hundreds of books and thousands of web pages. Millions of people across the globe (including me) are living better, happier lives because they practice and live mindfully. So can you.

If you are experiencing any sort of mental "push-back" against the idea of meditating, but at the same time would like to improve your mental wellbeing and enhance your life and the lives of those you love most, allow me to make a suggestion…

Set a routine—now, today.

This is the single most important step on your journey to living mindfully and developing your awareness. Set a time, morning and evening, for an appointment with yourself. Determine never to miss this appointment. When setting the times that you are going to meditate, be realistic: make sure it's doable. Give yourself every chance at success. Stick to this routine for six months and only then review what difference your practice has made in your life.

"Meditation practice isn't about trying to throw ourselves away and become something better. It's about befriending who we are already."
—Pema Chödrön

Everyday Mindfulness

Meditation practice is an important part of the development of mindfulness. The beneficial effect of our meditation doesn't stop when we get up from our "sitting," just as the benefit of exercise to our physical health doesn't stop as soon as we have finished exercising. Both carry over into our lives and contribute to our general wellbeing.

In order to truly engage our mindfulness practice, we have to incorporate mindful moments into our daily lives. Again, the idea is simple: the more mindful moments we have, the more mindfully we are living. Eventually, as you build up enough mindful moments, they will merge into mindful days—and before you know it, you are living mindfully! This is not about changing what you do every day, it's about being aware, bringing your full, mindful attention to what you are already doing as part of your daily routine. In the Everyday Mindfulness portions of this book, you'll find examples of how to turn routine tasks into mindful moments. These will give you ideas but you should look at your own routine and choose three or four tasks you do every day and practice carrying these out *mindfully*. Once you are doing them with awareness consistently, pick three or four more and start working on turning these into mindful moments.

Just a word here about mindfulness versus concentration. These are very different things, but are often confused with one another. Concentration is when you are focused single-mindedly on something. Mindfulness is the awareness that you are concentrating.

"Some people do not know the difference between "mindfulness" and "concentration." They concentrate on what they're doing, thinking that is being mindful. We can concentrate on what we are doing, but if we are not mindful at the same time, with the ability to reflect on the moment, then if somebody interferes with our concentration, we may blow up, get carried away by anger at being frustrated. If we are mindful, we are aware of the tendency to first concentrate and then to feel anger when something interferes with that concentration. With mindfulness, we can concentrate when it is appropriate to do so and not concentrate when it is appropriate not to do so."

—*Ajahn Sumedho*

Mindful Ideas

I've included some mindful ideas throughout the book, which I hope you find useful.

These are all things I have found to be beneficial to my practice, that have helped me live more mindfully. They are fun, and in my experience, if you do them regularly, they add a different, more relaxed quality to your life.

Enjoy!

"Mindful and creative, a child who has neither a past, nor examples to follow, nor value judgments, simply lives, speaks and plays in freedom."
—Arnaud Desjardins

1-Minute Mindfulness

In times of stress, anxiety, panic, or frustration we are not always in a position to sit quietly and meditate for five or ten minutes. There are lots of mindful techniques to help us in moments of turmoil and you'll find some of these in the 1-Minute Mindfulness exercises. I have included them specifically for times when you need to stop and back away, but where the situation you are in doesn't allow you to this.

It is important to note that these "quick fixes" for difficult situations are not the best way to deal with our suffering, which is caused primarily by our reactions to the strife life throws at us. The best solution is to build up your practice to the point where you are living mindfully, and in that way, you will have the awareness to avoid reacting in a way that causes suffering altogether. That said, these "quick fixes" will certainly make your life easier in the meantime.

"Mindfulness is the aware, balanced acceptance of the present experience. It isn't more complicated than that. It is opening to or receiving the present moment, pleasant or unpleasant, just as it is, without either clinging to it or rejecting it."
—*Sylvia Boorstein*

The Treasury

Mindful Idea – Create a Space

In many homes around the world, there is a room or a space reserved for quiet reflection. This is a great gift for you and your family. In my home, we have converted part of the spare room into a family sitting space, which is screened off from the rest of the room by one of those mobile room dividers. Our sitting space is small but uncluttered, containing only cushions and a lamp. My wife and I use it for our daily meditations and every Tuesday and Sunday we (my wife, our two boys aged eight and eleven, and I) gather here for our "family sitting." We start by assembling outside the door and take time to calm and quieten down before we enter. We take our seats on our cushions and spend a few moments listening to calming music and noticing our breathing. After that I usually lead a ten-minute guided meditation suitable for our children. Then, we listen to a story or teaching (in our home, it's usually a story based on Buddhist morals or ethics), making sure that it's fun and age-appropriate for our boys. Then we take a little time to talk about what we've learned. This is followed by a relaxing meditation in which we let go of all the tension in our bodies—and, if possible, the worries from our minds. Without speaking—except for a gentle "good night"—we put our boys to bed, and we head downstairs for a cup of tea and a chat.

I can honestly say that our two boys really enjoy our "family sitting" and it's not unusual to hear the younger one ask to have one on a Thursday or Friday evening as well! Having a space in our home for quiet reflection is wonderful for our family—and I know it will benefit you and your family too.

Here is an excerpt from Brother Phap Dung's New Year's Eve Talk, which he gave at Plum Village Monastery on December 31, 2017. I love his advice on how to use your quiet space:

> *A peace room, a spiritual room. A room where you dedicate to come back and to remember. That room can be empty of furniture. We have a living room, dining room, entertainment room,*

office room, a room for the car even! But we don't have a room for peace. We need a room for peace. Every time someone in the family has difficulty, they can go to that room, and once the door or the curtain is closed, there is peace. You cannot disturb the person inside, even if it's your child. So we go there and we breathe to come back to ourselves. Each home needs a room like that. If you do not have an extra room, make it a corner somewhere in the house. Put something there, perhaps it is a flower, perhaps it is a calligraphy or a photo. Something to remind you that there is something more important than just running around.

"Each morning we are born again. What we do today is what matters most."

—The Buddha

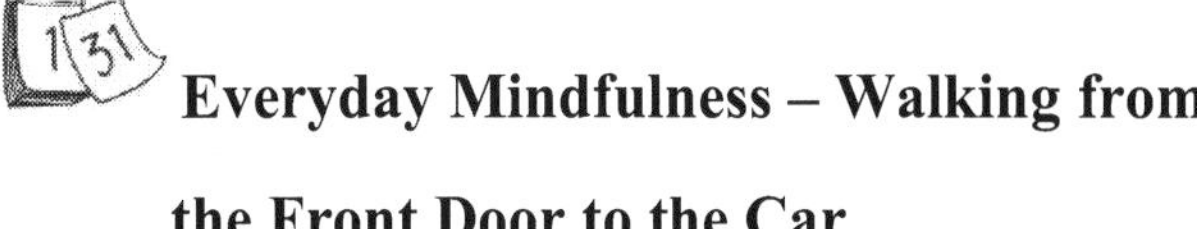

Everyday Mindfulness – Walking from the Front Door to the Car

This is something most of us do at least once every day. But can you actually remember doing it, can you remember the details of this short journey?

Making this a mindful moment is easy. Be aware of the weight of the door as you close it behind you and the feel of the key in your hand as you lock it. As you turn to walk to your car (or to the bus or train), pause for a moment. Look at the view in front of your house or apartment. Notice the movement of your legs as you walk, the sensation as your weight moves from one foot to the other. What sounds and smells can you recognise? Finally, observe the temperature and texture of the car door handle and the weight of the door as you open it.

Some people put a small mark just above their front door lock to remind them to do this exercise.

Mindful Meditation – Loving Kindness

Sit quietly on your cushion or chair, relax your body, and allow your eyes to close gently. Bring your focus and awareness to your breath wherever in your body you feel it most.

Call to mind someone you love and care for deeply. Allow a picture of them to form in your mind's eye. Remember why you feel so much love for this person and generate a feeling of love and kindness towards them. Then send them the following blessing. Really believe that your wish for them to be happy, healthy, and safe and to live with ease will have a direct effect on their lives.

May you be happy
May you be healthy
May you be safe
May you live with ease.

Now, realise that you are worthy and deserving of exactly the same in your own life.

Focus all your love and kindness on yourself. Make the same wish for yourself.

May I be happy
May I be healthy
May I be safe
May I live in peace.

Finally, picture all living beings everywhere and offer the same to them.

May they be happy
May they be healthy
May they be safe
May they live with ease.

Try this…
Whenever you think of or see someone who is suffering in any way—physically, mentally, or through whatever situation they may be in—generate

as much love and compassion as you can and silently send them this beautiful loving-kindness blessing. Be it a stranger, a homeless person on the street, or a couple arguing, remember that just like you, they want to be free from suffering. They want to be happy, healthy, and safe and they want to live with ease.

"The more we genuinely care about others, the greater our own happiness and inner peace."
—*Allan Lokos*

"Like a caring mother, holding and guarding the life of her only child, so with a boundless heart of loving kindness, hold yourself and all beings as your beloved children."

—*The Buddha*

"Be kind whenever possible. It is always possible."

—His Holiness, The 14th Dalai Lama

 Mindful Idea – Use the Tech

There is a plethora of apps and websites devoted to the topic of mindfulness. As always, some of the websites are better than others. I have found that those that don't try to make mindfulness complicated are the best. Search "mindfulness" online and have a look at the sites that come up.

As for apps, again you are spoiled for choice. Some of these are just meditation apps and offer different guided meditations. The most useful apps remind you to take mindful moments throughout the day. Such reminders can take the form of a gentle chime or an expanding circle on the screen, encouraging you to breathe mindfully. These are useful aids to building mindful moments into your day. Some apps are free, and even those that charge a fee often offer a free trial period. Download three of four that you like the look of and "road test" them for a while—then choose the one you find most beneficial. Even if you have to pay a small fee, it's generally well worth it. Two of my favourites are the “Plum Village App” and “Simple Habit”.

"Use everything and anything to conquer mindlessness."

—*Paddy Brosnan*

1-Minute Mindfulness – Breath

Take three deep, clearing breaths, breathing in deeply and out slowly through your nose.

Let your breath return to its normal rhythm and bring all your attention to the feel of your breath right at the tip of your nose. Be aware of the difference in temperature of your in-breath and out-breath. Notice that your in-breath is cool and your out-breath is warm. Allow your awareness to examine this difference for the next minute or so. On each inhale and exhale, see if you can determine if it is cooler/warmer than the last one.

"Begin doing what you want to do now. We are not living in eternity. We have only this moment, sparkling like a star in our hand—and melting like a snowflake."

—Francis Bacon

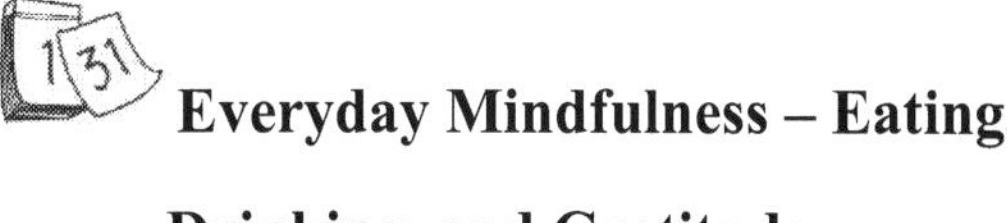

Everyday Mindfulness – Eating, Drinking, and Gratitude

Every day we must eat, every day we must drink, and every day we should be grateful. The fact that these are things we must or should do makes them excellent opportunities to practice mindfulness.

Not so long ago I was fortunate enough to be invited to lead a mindfulness retreat in a beautiful retreat centre in the south of Ireland. The morning was centred mostly around mindful meditation and as the session was drawing to a close, I informed the retreatants that we would be continuing our mindfulness practice during lunch. This announcement was met with a few low rumbles and grumbles and not so subtle moans and groans. I explained that we would be spending the first half of our lunch in complete silence, using this time to focus on our food and to practice mindful eating. This did not go down too well. One lady spoke boldly for the majority: "We've been practicing all morning; can we not have a break?" This reaction is understandable, but unfortunately, it misses the point.

Mindfulness is not something we do, it's something we are—or are striving to become. We should find every opportunity in our daily lives to practice mindfulness. The aim is not to spend fifteen or twenty minutes meditating and forget about it. The aim is to nurture our awareness so that we live mindfully—all the time!

Mindful Eating

To practice mindful eating, it's a good idea to be as silent as possible when we eat. Take a moment to look at your food before you start to eat, take in all the colours. Be aware of the weight of the cutlery in your hands and the smell of the food. When you put the food in your mouth, really taste it—is it hot or cold? Spicy? What's the texture? Chew your food well before you swallow.

Mindful Drinking

Mindful drinking is a wonderful habit to foster. Try to get into the habit of not holding your cup or mug by the handle. Instead, wrap your hands around the cup. Feel the warmth or coldness. Bring it to your mouth slowly, being aware and mindful of the movement. Breathe in the smell. Notice the feel of the cup or glass on your lips. Bring all your attention to the temperature and taste of the tea, coffee, or whatever you are drinking.

Mindful Gratitude

Mindful gratitude is something we could all practice and it's so simple. You just say what you're thankful for. So, instead of just saying "Thank you," you say: "Thank you for my meal" or "Thank you for holding the door." This simple practice reminds you what you're grateful for and gives the other person a better sense of your gratitude.

"It's only when we truly know and understand that we have a limited time on earth—and that we have no way of knowing when our time is up—that we will begin to live each day to the fullest, as if it was the only one we had."

—Elisabeth Kübler-Ross

Mindful Meditation – Thoughts

This meditation can sometimes be a little challenging. For this reason, I think some guidance is called for before you start.

In this practice, by learning to watch your thoughts come and go, you will see that they are transient by nature. You will also probably notice how some thoughts have emotions and desires caught up in them. This meditation practice can reveal our habitual thought patterns and our reactions to them. Most of the time this realisation will come as a surprise. By becoming aware of these patterns of thought, we can often liberate ourselves from old, stale ways of thinking.

I don't want you to get the idea that there is anything wrong with thoughts. Thinking makes up a large part of what the mind does—and it's normal and natural to think. The purpose of this meditation is not to stop thought or to restrict the thoughts we experience. The purpose is to observe our thoughts as part of our internal landscape, to learn that we don't have to believe or grasp onto every thought automatically. We can simply observe each thought as it arises, stays for a while, and leaves.

It might also be a good idea to get an understanding of what we mean when we talk about "thoughts." Thoughts can be internal dialogue or planning, and sometimes just random nonsense. Sometimes they can take the form of images, memories, daydreams, or fantasies. The feelings or emotions that accompany these make up the fabric of our thinking. Some thoughts are creative, some are destructive.

> With all this in mind, find a comfortable position on a cushion or chair. Try to keep your back straight and unsupported. Breathe in deeply and breathe out slowly through your nose. Allow your eyes to close gently.
>
> Take a moment and stay with your breath until it falls into a natural pattern and rhythm. Become aware of the sensation of breathing wherever you feel it most in your body. Allow

your attention to shift to the various thoughts that arise. Just observe your thoughts as they come and go, like clouds floating through a blue sky. Try not to get caught up in any thoughts. Simply observe thoughts as they come into your awareness, float through and pass away. Do not judge or resist any thoughts. Conversely, don't cling to any thoughts. Recognise every thought for what it is—just a thought that is not solid or real. Practice observing for a few minutes.

After a few minutes, investigate the thoughts you notice in a bit more detail. Are they images? Memories? Are they words and dialogue or plans? Do any emotions accompany any particular thought? Are there any associated feelings in your body? Are there gaps between the thoughts? If you find that this investigation has morphed into you being caught up in a thought or lost in its content, just note this has happened. Then return to observing the thoughts as they come and go. It is common and normal to get caught up in your thoughts. When this happens, be gentle with yourself. Congratulate yourself for noticing. If at any point this meditation practice becomes disturbing or you become distressed, switch your focus away from thought and onto whatever sounds you hear. Once you feel calmer, gently return to observing your thoughts.

When your allotted time is up, stay seated for a minute or two, bringing your attention to your breathing or to sounds in the space you are in. Then, slowly open your eyes.

Try this…

During the day, when you realise that you have been lost in thought, note that this has been the case. Congratulate yourself for noticing. Then bring your attention to the sensation of your breath for a few moments.

"When the mind is full of memories and preoccupied by the future, it misses the freshness of the present moment. In this way, we fail to recognize the luminous simplicity of mind that is always present behind the veils of thought."

—Matthieu Ricard

"The mind in its natural state can be compared to the sky, covered by layers of cloud which hide its true nature."

—Kalu Rinpoche

Everyday Mindfulness – Sweeping the Floor

Monks and Nuns in Buddhist monasteries around the world consider being asked to do this "chore" as a great opportunity to develop their awareness. They see it as a beautiful, graceful mindfulness exercise. This is a bit different to how the rest of us see sweeping the floor. I see their point though … if it's not rushed, there is something graceful about the motion of sweeping.

Pay attention to the feel and texture of the brush handle. Really notice what it feels like. Listen to the sound of the brush as it moves across the floor. Note the sensations involved in each movement of your body as you sweep. Slow down the movement a little to allow yourself time to absorb yourself in the task.

Forgetfulness is the enemy of mindfulness, so you might want to write the letter "M" on the head of the brush to remind you.

1-Minute Mindfulness – Doodle

Doodling is often seen as a waste of time, but it can be a great 1-minute mindfulness practice.

Feel the weight of the pen or pencil in your hand; be aware that you are holding it. Start to draw on the paper without any predetermined idea of what you are going to draw. Allow your mind to relax and simply enjoy the process of doing something unplanned. Get engrossed in your doodling!

When your minute or so is up, spend a little time looking at what you've created before moving on.

Mindful Idea – The Joy of Not Doing

Our modern society is obsessed with the notion of being busy. We wear our busy-ness as a badge of honour, and somehow see it as good thing. In this we are deluded, like the players of an augmented reality video game looking for imaginary creatures. Running and running, with nothing real to show for our efforts, we end up tired and worn out, and no better off at the end of it all. Friends and even partners try to constantly "out-busy" one another, often making the other person feel ashamed because they haven't done as much and aren't as busy. In reality, a lot of this busy-ness is a waste of time. What we are really doing is accepting blindly that this is the way we should be, that this is how we should live our lives. It isn't.

When you live mindfully with awareness, you see this folly for what it is. You will be able to see when enough has been done. Furthermore, you will be able to experience the joy of not doing. Not doing is different from putting things off or being lazy, it's the conscious act of deciding if something actually needs to be done or if it's just being done for the sake of doing something. It's knowing when you are physically and mentally tired, deciding that you have done enough, and that it's time for rest. Not doing is self-care. It's as important as doing, and knowing when and how to do both is important. I encourage you to question your busy-ness constantly and to rest mindfully.

"Time you enjoy wasting is not wasted time."

—Marthe Troly-Curtin

 Mindful Idea – The Phone and the ATM

The Phone

If you phone a Buddhist monastery (I single out Buddhist monasteries here, because mindfulness comes from Buddhism, and all Buddhist monastics practice mindfulness), you will most likely find that the phone will ring for a while before it's answered. This is not necessarily due to the monks and nuns being busy. Almost always, they are sitting quietly, listening to the phone ring.

In a monastic setting, a bell ringing is a call to mindfulness. So, as you wait for the phone to be answered, the monks or nuns have stopped whatever they were doing and are taking a moment to be aware of their breathing. When they have finished their "mindful moment," they will say "thank you" to whomever was kind enough to make the phone ring and provide them with an opportunity to practice mindfulness. Only then they will answer the phone.

This probably explains why Buddhist monastics always sound so happy when they answer the phone!

You can use this same technique in your own daily routine. When your phone rings or alerts you to a message or email, don't go to it straight away. Instead, take a moment. Focus all your awareness on the sensation of your next three breaths. This allows you a mindful moment, before you tend to your phone. You don't have to stop everything, and nobody needs to know you are spending a few seconds practicing mindful breathing. If you consider how often you interact with your phone, you can see how many opportunities this simple habit will give you to help you to build your mindfulness practice. As we know, all those mindful moments add up!

The ATM

A few years ago, a friend of mine asked me to help him find practical ways to enable him to remember to be mindful. We had a chat about his day, and it turned out he spent a lot of his time walking around the city centre. I suggested that he use the many ATMs he passed as a reminder to practice mindful walking. So, every time he passed an ATM, he focused his attention on the sensation of taking his next five steps. He used the same technique as described in the Mindful Movement Meditation in this book, consciously being aware of every movement involved in walking.

Can you think of anything in your day-to-day life that you could use as a reminder for you to take five mindful steps?

“In today’s rush, we all think too much, seek too much, want too much and forget about the joy of just Being.”

—Eckhart Tolle

"There are only two ways to live your life. One is as though nothing is a miracle. The other is as though everything is a miracle."
—Albert Einstein

1-Minute Mindfulness – Tension Release

Tightening—then relaxing—one muscle group at time is an excellent way to relieve stress and is a wonderful mindfulness exercise.

Start by tensing the muscles of your face and neck, scrunching up the face, and tightening the neck. Hold this for a few moments and notice what it feels like. Then, relax your muscles as you slowly breathe out. Be aware of the changing sensations in your face and neck as you relax and breathe out.

Move on to your belly and lower back. Tense your muscles by sucking in your belly to make it flatter. Hold. Note what this feels like. Breathe out and relax the tension in this area, being sensitive to the difference this makes.

Continue the exercise by clenching, tightening, and releasing your buttocks and then the calves of your legs. Finish by curling your toes to tighten the muscles in your feet and then relaxing the tension. Tense each muscle group for a length of time that is slightly uncomfortable—but never until it becomes painful. Be mindful of how each muscle group reacts when you breathe out and loosen up the tension.

Mindful Meditation – Breathing

Sit quietly on your chair or cushion. Make sure your back is straight and unsupported.

Take a few deep breaths in through your nose and release your breath slowly through your nose. Let your eyes close.

Bring your awareness to the sensation of your breath as it enters your nose and leaves your nose. Just focus on the sensation of your breath at the tip of your nose. When you're ready, expand your focus to include the entire cycle of your breath. Notice the air entering your nose, then the sensation of your chest expanding, then your belly expanding. Notice also the little pause before your belly deflates, then your chest and finally, the sensation of your breath leaving the tip of your nose. Practice following the sensation of the breathing process for a few moments.

It's important not to try to make it a special breath or to control your breath in any way. You are breathing, so just focus and be aware of what is happening naturally. Simply be aware of your breathing as it is happening. Don't think about your last breath or anticipate your next breath, simply be with this breath that's happening now. It sometimes helps to count each cycle of your breath quietly to yourself. Mentally count every in- and out-breath as one cycle. Count each breath one to ten and when you reach ten, begin to count the next ten breaths in reverse, from ten to one. Then start at one again … and so on.

Remember to congratulate yourself when you notice that your mind has wandered away from your breath. Gently direct your attention away from wherever your mind has gone and back to focusing on your breath. Wherever your mind had gone—thinking, planning, or just daydreaming—there will be plenty of time for that later. Right now, you are paying attention to your breath. Nothing else.

When your time is up, open your eyes. Sit still for a few moments. Try to bring the experience of being aware of the cycle of your breath with you throughout your day. You don't have to sit and close your eyes to focus on your breath. You can do this at any time, regardless of whatever else you may be doing. So, try to remember to use this beautiful, calming practice as many times as you can as you go through your day.

Try this…

Often, we find ourselves in situations that annoy us. This leads us to suffer with frustration, even anger. Stuck in traffic that's making us late for an appointment, standing in a queue, stuck on the phone with a customer service agent who's providing anything but customer service—we all experience situations like these. Deep down, we know there is nothing we can do about these things, but that doesn't stop our reactive mind from kicking in. When this happens, annoyance, frustration, and anger soon follow—and of course they do nothing to fix the situation. Sitting in your car fuming will not make traffic move. Shouting at your partner because they forgot to pick up the dry cleaning will not get it home any quicker. The only outcome is mental suffering for us and for others.

The next time you feel annoyance or frustration welling up, try to catch it before it takes over, before the reactive mind kicks in. Acknowledge that negative reactions will do nothing to make the situation better. Say to yourself: "I'm starting to feel angry/annoyed/frustrated, but I know that won't help me." Then go to the sensation of your breath and focus your attention and awareness on the in-and-out cycle of your breathing, just like you did in meditation. When your mind tries to jump back to the situation you're in, gently bring it back to your breath. Take refuge in your breath until your reactive mind has settled and the feelings that come with it have passed. Taking refuge in your breath may seem like an odd concept. But one main reason we practice focusing on the breath in meditation is so that we can use it in times of emotional turmoil. We build up our "meditation muscles" to the point where centring on our breathing is a natural reaction to the onslaught of suffering caused by detrimental, reactive feelings.

"Feelings come and go like clouds in a windy sky. Conscious breathing is my anchor."
—Thich Nhat Hanh

"If you want to conquer the anxiety of life, live in the moment, live in the breath."

—*Amit Ray*

Mindful Idea – Mindful Hands and Happy Hair

Take some hand cream and apply it to your hands. Gently massage the cream into your skin and focus some of your attention on your breathing. Start with the little finger of one hand and move along, massaging and moisturising each finger and eventually the thumb. Be aware of any sensations that occur and how different it feels from one finger to the next. Is the baby finger more sensitive? Is the thumb less sensitive? Move on to the palm of your hand, then the back of your hand, again noticing differences in texture and sensitivity. When you have completely nourished and massaged one hand, repeat the ritual on your other hand.

Notice every detail you. What does the cream feel like when you first apply it? Focus. Be aware of how it feels as you massage and moisturise each finger and each part of your hand. What does the hand cream smell like? Do you notice any sounds?

Allow your mind to be fully present and engaged with what you are doing.

When you're finished, take a moment to consider how valuable our hands are and how much they do for us.

Brushing your hair is another opportunity to practice mindfulness and to take a mindful moment or two for yourself. As with all the other examples of daily mindfulness, this is something you do anyway. The only difference is that now you are fully aware of your actions, turning something that might have been a chore into a pleasant, calming experience.

As you brush your hair, become aware of the movement of your arm and hand and the weight of the brush. Notice what your scalp feels like as the brush passes over it. Have the muscles in your neck become tense? What does it feel like as the brush passes through your hair? Can you detect any smell? If you come across a tangle, be aware of any tension in your arm or face. Be present for the whole experience.

Making the effort to be consciously aware of what we are doing as we are doing it focuses our mind. This is a wonderful practice—if our mind is focused on moisturising our hands or brushing our hair, it can't be off worrying or regretting or some other pointless activity that causes suffering.

Note:

If the publisher has been unwise enough to include a picture of me in this book, you will see that I do not have flowing locks on which I can practice mindful brushing. My wife, whom I am happy to report is not in the least follicly challenged, kindly provided the last example.

"Altogether, the idea of meditation is not to create states of ecstasy or absorption, but to experience being."

—Chögyam Trungpa

Everyday Mindfulness – Washing dishes

Listen to the sound of the water filling the sink. Notice the smell of the washing-up liquid as it mixes with the water. Make sure your full attention is on the task at hand. Sense the temperature of the water and the slightly slippery texture it has from the detergent. Pay attention to the weight of the different types of crockery and cutlery as you handle them and the movement of your hands as you clean the dishes.

If your mind wanders, gently bring it back to washing the dishes. If your mind wants you to focus on something else, you can silently say, “There will be time for that later. Now I am washing the dishes.”

"We have only now, only this single eternal moment opening and unfolding before us, day and night."
—Jack Kornfield

Mindful Meditation – Choiceless Awareness

This choiceless awareness meditation (sometimes called open awareness) needs a little instruction before you start.

As the name suggests, when you practice this meditation you don't choose where to place your awareness. You just note whatever you become aware of. To make this a little easier, we use three words— "thought," "feeling" and "sensation." So, if a thought like, "I don't think I'm doing this right" or "I must remember to get milk later" has your attention, you simply note silently: "thought." If you become aware of a feeling like happy, confused, bored, or delighted, you just say silently: "feeling." Likewise, if you feel a sensation like a sound or a smell or an itch or ache, you just note its presence by silently saying: "sensation."

The idea is simple. Just sit and note whatever comes to your awareness using three words: thought, feeling, or sensation. The intention is to just observe without judgement whatever passes through your awareness. A word of caution, though. This is probably the easiest meditation to get lost in—we can find ourselves daydreaming or being carried away quickly by thought instead of just observing. When this happens, gently bring yourself back to choiceless awareness and start again.

Let's begin.

Find a quiet place where you won't be disturbed. Take your meditation position and breathe through your nose until you are relaxed and calm.

Allow your attention to settle wherever it chooses and note what you are aware of. If it's a thought, say "thought" silently … or say "sensation" if it's a sensation or "feeling" if you are aware of a feeling. Just note whatever you are experiencing moment by moment. Sometimes it can be difficult to decide if it's a thought or feeling you are aware of. If this is the case, just note it as "thought/feeling." Don't become distracted. Remember, this is an exercise in simply observing whatever passes through your consciousness, not an exercise in absolute precision. Just sit and watch, as one thought is replaced by another thought, or by a feeling followed by a sensation or another thought. The content or tone of what arises is not important, so don't get caught up in it. Watch as each thought, feeling, or sensation appears and fades.

As I said, if you find you have drifted off and are caught up instead of just observing, bring yourself back gently to choiceless, open awareness. You may have to do this a few times, so don't get disheartened. Some people experience a rapid pace of change between thoughts, sensations, and feelings when they first practice this meditation—a bit like watching a movie on fast forward. If you experience this and find it hard to keep pace with your mental noting, please stick with it. The pace will slow down in a short while.

When your time is up, sit quietly for a few moments with your eyes open, and reflect on your meditation.

Try this…

After four or five days of practicing choiceless awareness, see if you can notice a difference in how you relate to your thoughts and feelings in your everyday life. Are you reacting less to situations? Are you aware of thoughts that might have gone unnoticed before? Are you choosing whether or not to act on thoughts or feelings, instead of reacting blindly?

"Meditation is to be aware of what is going on: in your body, in your feelings, in your mind, and in the world."

—Thich Nhat Hanh

"When you are present, you can allow the mind to be as it is without getting entangled in it."
—Eckhart Tolle

Mindful Idea – Use the Yellow Squares

Post-it notes can be your best friend on your journey to living mindfully.

Put one on your bathroom mirror and draw teeth on it, to remind yourself to be mindful when you brush your teeth.

Write "feet" on one and put it beside your alarm clock. This will remind you to be aware of the feel of your feet on the floor when you get out of bed, just before you stand up. This little mindful pause will also give you the opportunity to be thankful for another day.

Put a Post-it note on the handles of the doors you use most often—with the letter M written on each one. This will serve as a reminder to be aware of the movement in your arm as you reach out and open the door.

If you work at a desk, put a Post-it on the seat of your chair. You'll hear it crinkle when you sit down. This will remind you to bring your awareness to the feel of your body on the chair for a few moments each time you take your seat.

Put a Post-it on the dashboard of your car. You'll see this each time you get behind the wheel. This is your reminder to sit for a moment before you start your car and to bring all your attention to the feel of the steering wheel in your hands.

This is just a small sample of the kinds of things we do every day, sometimes many times a day. It may seem like too much effort to try to engage with these mundane tasks in a mindful way—but think of how many times a day you sit down or open a door. Now consider how many mindful moments you could build up in a typical day if you performed these tasks with awareness every time.

Spend a moment to write down any activities you do repeatedly every day and how you are going to remind yourself to do these mindfully.

"When we rush in with this mental chatter, we are no longer being mindful. We are just thinking about being mindful. Mindfulness is not thinking about, it is being present and actually knowing in the moment without any mental commentary."
—*Ani Tenzin Palmo*

Everyday Mindfulness – Traffic, Queue, On Hold

Throughout the day, you will be presented with events and experiences that could, if you let them, bother and annoy you. Some of the most common among these are being stuck in traffic, waiting in a queue, or being put on hold on the phone.

Obviously, how you view these events is a matter of perception. In our western society, we have a terrible habit of catastrophising even the smallest upsets. Waiting in a queue is often used as an opportunity to confirm that we are having a bad day. As soon as we see the queue, we think, "Ahh, can this day get any worse?" Most of the time, if we review our day up to that point, nothing bad has actually happened—but now, because we have to queue, we use the event to paint the entire day as "bad."

The same can be said for being stuck in traffic or being put on hold on the phone. When you think about it … it's bizarre! Bizarre, but understandable … because we fall into old patterns of thought. Automatically, we're carried to annoyance, anger, or frustration. We react. We don't stop to consider whether our reactions and the feelings generated are proportional to the event taking place. At this point we are living mindlessly, not mindfully—and we suffer the unpleasant feelings.

Make a conscious decision to use events that would normally annoy you as triggers to remind you: *Be mindful.* When you see the queue or the traffic, treat these exactly the same as you would any other reminder to be mindful. Bring your attention to the sensation of your breath, or to the sounds you hear. Stay with this for a few moments, noticing everything you can about your breath or the sounds in a curious, matter-of-fact way, without labelling or judging—but simply noticing. Now, use the precious gift of spare time that the queue or traffic has given you to bring joy to your day. Call to mind all the good things that have happened to you recently. Focus your attention mindfully on any positive experiences you have had. Reflect on how you are grateful for these and other things—like your health, friends, partner, and family.

This mindful focusing on joy is a lot more beneficial to your mental wellbeing and overall mood than the usual, default reaction of annoyance or anger. The length of time you spend on hold or in traffic will be exactly the same, no matter how you decide to use it. By making this time an opportunity to practice mindfulness and appreciation, you use it well and for your own benefit.

“The next time you are stuck in traffic, you might want to reflect on the fact that to others, you are also traffic.”

—Paddy Brosnan

1-Minute Mindfulness – Mind Games

Our brains are hardwired to notice and remember negative events and information. If you're having a stressful day, odds are that your brain is replaying those stressful events long after the stress has passed. Mental games are fun brain activities that help you refocus.

- Count backwards by seven, starting at 1007.
- Create a sentence where every word must begin with the same letter. For example, "All avocados are awkward." Then go onto, "Betsy's big ball bounces beautifully."
- List as many song titles as you can by your favourite artist.
- Pick a location within walking distance and mentally map the shortest/longest route.

Mindful Meditation – Gratitude

Sit quietly, with your back straight. Allow your body to relax. Bring your awareness to the sensation of your breath as it enters and leaves your nose. Notice the rise and fall of your chest. Where do you feel it the most?

Now call to mind all those who have helped you through your life and see if you can allow a picture of the person to form in your mind: *your parents … your teachers* ... say "Thank you" to each one as they pass through your mind's eye … *family members ... friends ... doctors ... partners, past and present ... strangers who showed you kindness.*

We all have people in our lives who have supported us in the past or are supporting us now. Allow a warm glow of protection to surround you as you remember the many people who have helped you up to this point. Generate a deep sense of gratitude towards each of them for their kindness.

Spend a moment contemplating how many people are involved in helping you every day … from the people who grow and distribute your food … to the people who provide the many services you use, like water, electricity, roads, and waste disposal. We couldn't live our lives without an army of people to help us. Take a moment to appreciate the vast numbers of people involved in supporting your life. Allow yourself time to contemplate this incredible inter-connectedness.

Try this…

During the day, notice the people around you who are working on your behalf: the delivery man driving alongside you in his truck, the utility workers repairing a leak at the side of the road, the postal service worker diligently delivering to each address. The server at the restaurant who brought your food and the cook who prepared it. The police, ambulance, and fire brigade, keeping you safe. The sanitation service people collecting the refuse and the street sweeper who makes sure you have a pleasant environment to enjoy.

As you notice each of these individuals, say a warm "Thank You."

"At times, our own light goes out and is rekindled by a spark from another person. Each of us has cause to think with deep gratitude of those who have lighted the flame within us."
—Albert Schweitzer

"The more grateful I am, the more beauty I see."

—*Mary Davis*

Mindful Meditation – Sight

Meditation on What You See

Position yourself in front of a window, preferably in your meditation posture, either on a cushion or on a chair. Look at and notice everything there is to see. Take in the whole view. Try not to label what you see: "bird" or "tree" or "car." Try to drop all labels. Try also to drop all emotive judgements, like "pretty" or "weird" or "I don't like." Just see the scene in front of you without labels or opinions.

Notice as much detail as you can in the slice of the world you see through the window. Be curious. Inspect the colours and shapes, the light and shadows. Be aware of movement in the grass, plants, or trees; of the birds, animals, or people you see. Remember to check constantly that you are not labelling (for example: "person"). Instead, investigate the details of what you see. It can be useful during this meditation to adopt the attitude of someone who has never seen any of the things you are looking at before. Check that you do not become fixated on any one particular thing or aspect. Let your attention be drawn to whatever takes its interest.

If you find yourself getting lost in thought or wandering off to planning or daydreaming, just bring your focus and awareness to your breath. From there start your "meditation on what you see" again. When your meditation is finished, go to awareness of your breath for a few moments before you move on.

Meditation on an Object

This meditation is usually practiced with a predetermined object as your focus. Normally, you use a lit candle—but you can use other things, like a leaf dancing in the wind, or grass swaying. Some people like to use an image or statue of a spiritual figure important to them, like the Buddha or Jesus. For the purposes of this meditation, I will use the example of a lit candle, but the principle is the same whatever object you use.

Sit quietly in meditation position with your eyes open but focused on nothing in particular. Slowly focus on the candle. Start in the middle of the stem of the candle. Notice its shape. Can you define any texture, grooves, or bumps? Are there areas of light or shadow visible? Move your attention and focus up the candle, slowly, noticing any details you come across along the way.

Now allow your awareness to settle on the flame. Be aware of the different colours at the base, middle, and top. Notice any change in colour as you inspect each area in turn. Does the colour change … sometimes white, yellow, or maybe blue? Focus on the flame as a whole. Notice how it changes in size one moment to the next. Be aware of changes in the intensity of the flickering light, how its brightness blooms and diminishes from moment to moment.

A word of caution might be required here. While watching a lit candle, it is easy to drift off into daydreaming. So, during this beautiful meditation, make sure you haven't zoned out, that you are concentrating fully on the flame and the changes happening within it. If your mind drifts to unrelated thoughts, gently bring it back to where you want it to be. Notice any inclination to turn your head in search of something more interesting. Then return to examining the flickering candle mindfully.

When the time comes to end your meditation, close your eyes. Imagine the warm glow of the candle wrapping your body gently with its nourishing warmth. Stay with this feeling for a few moments before opening your eyes and continuing on with your day.

"Your vision will become clear only when you look into your heart. Who looks outside, dreams. Who looks inside, awakens."
—Carl Jung

Mindful Meditation – Pleasant Moment

Get yourself into a comfortable position. When you're ready, allow your eyes to close. It's important to be comfortable and relaxed during this practice, so spend a few moments getting your position right and release any tension you might feel.

Gently settle into your body, allowing your body to become flexible and slightly heavy at the same time. Allow your awareness to gather around the movement and sensations of the breath in your whole body.

As you focus on the sensations within your body, let your attention be drawn to anything pleasant or enjoyable. What do you discover? Maybe the sensation of one hand resting in the other is pleasant, maybe your body is warm—is this pleasant? Can you get a sense of enjoyment from the general relaxed nature of your body as you practice? Bring a gentle, kind curiosity to your awareness as you pay attention to subtle and quiet experiences as well as strong ones.

What about sounds? Maybe there's a pleasant sound inside or outside the room—or maybe you're in a quiet place and that's comforting.

Are there any nice smells in your environment?

Explore these enjoyable sensations with curiosity, for as long as feels comfortable. Allow a smile to form in recognition of what you are experiencing.

Spend time resting in this broad awareness, allowing anything pleasant to come and go—enjoying it, appreciating it, staying open to the changing nature of this type of practice. Don't try to grasp any particular experience, just let it subside and be replaced by another.

When you are ready, gently open your eyes. Be aware of anything pleasing you see that brings you joy. Let your gaze wander softly around the room.

Finally, move your body a little, enjoying the sensation of movement that comes after a period of stillness. In your own time, go on about your day, bringing this awareness of your pleasant experience with you.

 1-Minute Mindfulness – Slack Jaw

This might seem like an unusual exercise, but it's precisely its unusualness that makes it effective.

Release the tension in your jaw, let it drop and become slack. Your mouth can open slightly or remain loosely closed. For the next minute or so, let your attention rest on how this feels. Be curious about the changing sensations moment to moment. Can you feel stress and tension in the rest of your body being released?

"Mindfulness is not just a word or a teaching by the Buddha, but a meaningful state of mind. It means we have to be here now, in this very moment, and we have to know what is happening internally and externally. It means being alert to our motives and learning to change unwholesome thoughts and emotions into wholesome ones. Mindfulness is a mental activity that in due course eliminates all suffering."

—*Ayya Khema*

Everyday Mindfulness – Who's in Your Shower?

For the vast majority of you kind and beautiful people reading this book, it is highly probable that you only rarely shower alone!

"What?" I hear you cry. Don't worry, I'm not judging you. (We Buddhists try hard not to judge, you know.) It's just a fact that most people bring a whole legion of people into their shower with them on most days. For instance, everyone who annoyed you the day before or the people you have to encounter in the day to come are in the shower with you. The irony is, given the choice, you wouldn't choose to share your shower, physically, with any of these people, but you are happy to take them along with you in your head. Lost in thought, planning and catastrophising, the last thing you are doing is having a shower. What a waste of a great opportunity to experience something truly relaxing—and a little bit decadent.

So, from this day forward, make a resolution that you will shower alone!

Having a shower presents us with the perfect opportunity to bring our mind, body, and environment together and in doing so, to be truly present and mindful of what we are experiencing. Feel the water on your body, the temperature, the intensity—be fully aware. Smell the soap or shower gel and notice how the smell undergoes subtle changes constantly. Feel the texture of the sponge or cloth, experience how this feels on different parts of your body. Notice and be aware of the sounds. Bring all your focus to the present moment and to what you are aware of in that moment. When your mind wanders off, notice where it has gone and say to yourself, "Thank you, but I'm having a shower now. I'll deal with that later." Then focus your mind back on your shower. Do this whenever your mind wanders, eventually it will stop.

It might seem like a small thing, but by having a mindful shower you will have built ten or fifteen minutes of mindful awareness into your day. You will also experience joy and have peace of mind for the time you spend showering. Most importantly, you will learn that bringing mindfulness to the everyday things we do feels good, and that the world did not fall apart because you didn't spend this time thinking and worrying.

Mindful Idea – A Mindful Day

I want to let you know about a new year's resolution I made some years ago, that turned out to be one of the few I ever stuck with. This was the simple resolution to have one mindful day as often as I could. As it turned out, I loved my mindful days so much that they soon became a weekly occurrence.

I first came across the idea of having one mindful day a week from the teachings of the Zen Buddhist monk, Thich Nhat Hanh. Thich Nhat Hanh is a Buddhist monk, author, and global spiritual leader. He introduced the practice of mindfulness to the West around the time of the Vietnam war and was nominated for a Nobel Peace Prize.

Here is my take on what he suggests….

Try this.

Pick a day that is not going to be full of things to do … maybe a day when you are not working and there isn't a lot of family stuff to be done. Put a reminder beside your bed the night before in a place where you will see it the moment you wake up. It can be a note or a picture, whatever you like.

Before you get out of bed, spend a few moments lying there. Bring your focus to the sensation of your breath as your chest rises and falls. Allow a smile to form on your face and let your body to relax. Get out of bed gently and as your feet touch the floor, be aware of that sensation and all the other sensations in your body as you stand up. Stand in place for a moment and say to yourself, "Today is my mindfulness day and I am happy." Then, do your morning mindful meditation if this is part of your normal routine.

Go about your usual morning activities, remembering to be mindful. As you shower, be aware of the feel of the water on your body, the smell of the soap or shower gel. While brushing your teeth, bring your attention to the feel of the brush on your teeth and gums. Drink your tea or coffee and eat your breakfast mindfully, focusing on the smells, tastes, temperature, and textures.

From here let your day develop and flow naturally, with as little planning as possible. When the "have to thoughts" like "I have to do…" or "I have to go…" come to your mind, take a moment before acting on them. Check that they are actually true. Do you really "have to" do whatever it is right now, or can it wait until tomorrow? Don't get pushed around by these thoughts, question them. Allow your day to unfold organically, remembering to make sure that your mind is focused on whatever you are doing in that moment. Bring the practice and energy of mindfulness to everything you do. If you decide to go for a walk, make sure you are aware of the movement of your feet and legs as you walk. What sounds can you hear? What scents are in the air? What is the quality of the light around you? You might like to get some house cleaning done. Instead of rushing through this task, bring a mindful quality to it. Simply ensure that your attention is on whatever you are doing—vacuuming, dusting, sweeping—and that your mind is engaged in that task and not wandering off. When you interact with other people, be present for them. Listen to what they are saying and don't allow your mind to stray onto what you are going to say next. When you speak, be cognisant of your words and any negative impact they might have.

In the evening, set aside some quiet time to read, to listen to music, or to sit in mindful meditation, whatever gentle activity you like doing by yourself. As you lie in bed before you go to sleep, be grateful for the day you just had and the opportunity to live a whole day with ease.

I love my mindful days because they are completely free of stress and schedules, I allow them to just … unfold. There is a huge sense of freedom and contentment in this. The main barrier to having a day like this is that most of us feel we just won't be able to set aside a whole day. The beauty of this idea is that you are not setting "aside" a day to be mindful, you are doing whatever you would normally do, but you are doing it mindfully, with attention. The other benefit is that you will avoid the nonsense of "false busy-ness" … that sense that you *have to* do this or go here or go there. When you question these impulses, you'll find that most times they aren't true. Rejecting them will allow you precious time to relax, without that anxious feeling of having to rush to the next thing. After just a few mindful days, you'll find that this "relaxed, not rushing" attitude will find its way into your "normal" days as well.

"Life is really simple, but we insist on making it complicated."
—*Confucius*

Everyday Mindfulness – Speaking

Try to be aware of what you are saying, whether it's face-to-face with someone or on the telephone. Listen actively to what you are saying and how you are saying it. What tone are you using? At what volume are you speaking? Is what you're saying necessary or are you just speaking for the sake of it?

This is a beautiful practice, because what you say and how you say it can have an enormous effect on others and on you. Becoming mindful of what you are saying will make it a lot more likely that people will want to listen to and talk to you.

When we speak, normally we concentrate only on the content of what we are saying, not on the affect our words might have. If you practice speaking mindfully, you will force yourself to be aware of all the aspects of your words. This focus on what you are saying, how you're saying it, and what affect it might have inevitably will make you a kinder person. When you become good at being mindful of what you say, your words will naturally pass through the three filters: Is what I am saying kind? Is it necessary? Is it true?

"Speak only if it improves upon the silence."

—*Gandhi*

Mindful Meditation – Sound

Sit quietly on your chair or cushion and allow your eyes to close.

Bring your attention to the tip of your nose and the sensation of your breath entering and leaving. Allow your attention to rest gently on this sensation for a few moments.

Now allow the focus of your attention to change and become aware of the sounds you hear. Be aware of sounds that are near as well as distant sounds. Just spend a few moments hearing.

Now notice how the sounds come and go by themselves. You don't have to do anything. They arise in your awareness, stay for a while, and fade, replaced by another sound or by silence. Spend time noticing this parade of sound through your awareness. Try not to judge any sound as good or bad, pleasant, or irritating. Don't focus on or hang onto “pleasant” sounds or dismiss “unpleasant” sounds. Just let them come and go.

Your mind will wander, and that’s okay. We are gently retraining your mind. It will want to do what it has always done naturally: plan, worry, focus on aches and itches, and generally wander away from where you want it to be (which is focused on the sounds you hear). When you notice that your mind has strayed to thoughts or feelings etc., congratulate yourself for recognising this. Then gently bring your attention back to being aware of the sounds you hear. This noticing that your mind has wandered and bringing it back may happen a lot in the beginning. That’s okay, because the more your mind wanders, the more opportunities you have to bring it back to where you want it to be. That’s the point, the essence of this meditation.

When your time for meditating is up, allow your eyes to open slowly. Spend a few moments just sitting still and allowing yourself a little time to transition from your meditation.

Try this…

The next time you are walking, try practicing this mindful meditation on sound. It doesn't have to be a special walk, you can practice while walking anywhere—to the bus or train, to your car, along the beach or in nature, or just down the street: it doesn't matter. As you set out, bring your attention to the sensation of your breath wherever you feel it most—perhaps in your nostrils, chest, or belly. Then gently allow your awareness to focus on hearing the sounds around you. Let these sounds come and go, just as you do in your sitting meditation. As before, when you notice your mind has drifted, bring it back gently to hearing.

When you reach your destination, you will be calm and relaxed and a lot less stressed than usual. You'll realise that you don't need to spend your walking time caught up in thinking and planning and worrying. You can just spend your time walking and hearing—which is probably much more beneficial to your mental wellbeing!

Even though you can practice this "walking-hearing" anywhere, when practiced in nature, it is an incredibly nurturing and beautiful experience. Make some time to take a stroll in a woodland or in the park and practice your meditation on sound as you go.

"All sounds of the earth are like music."

—Oscar Hammerstein

"Simply notice that you're aware. At any given moment, you can choose to follow the chain of thoughts, emotions, and sensations that reinforce a perception of yourself as vulnerable and limited, or to remember that your true nature is pure, unconditioned, and incapable of being harmed."
—*Yongey Mingyur Rinpoche*

 Mindful Idea – Do What You Love to Do

Doing something mindfully is simply bringing awareness to what you are doing. It's about bringing the three magic elements together—body, mind, and environment. The body and environment are not so difficult, but the mind likes to wander, and often, we are happy to allow it to do so. This is despite the fact that seldom does it wander to anywhere useful (often, in fact, it goes somewhere unhelpful). Our wandering mind also robs us of the opportunity to be engaged fully with our lives. We miss whole chunks of our days because we are lost in useless thought. This wayward mindlessness robs us of the extraordinary joy that can be found in the simplest things we do every day.

We all have things we love to do, that bring us joy. It might be gardening, taking a walk in nature, reading a book, spending time with family and friends, or going to concerts or live sports events. The next time you are doing whatever it is you love to do, decide to do it with complete awareness: give it your full attention. If you're at a concert, take in the atmosphere, notice the people around you and their excitement. If it's gardening you love, bring your awareness consciously to the smells and the colours around you; feel the temperature and texture of the soil you are working with. You will be amazed how much this enhanced alertness to the present moment will change your experience. When you bring the energy of mindfulness to something you already love doing, the joy is multiplied, and you will find a place where you flourish.

Please don't just take my word for it. Put this book down and go do whatever it is you truly enjoy. Do it mindfully, bringing mind, body, and environment together. Experience the difference for yourself!

"It's a helluva start, being able to recognize what makes you happy."

—Lucille Ball

1-Minute Mindfulness – Senses

Notice five things you can **see**.

Look around you. Bring your attention to five things you see. Pick something you wouldn't notice normally … like a shadow … or maybe an insect on a wall.

Notice four things you can **feel**.

Be aware of four things you are feeling right now … like the texture of your clothes, the feeling of the air on your skin, or the surface of a table.

Notice three things you can **hear**.

Take a moment to listen and note three things you hear. Try to focus on sounds that are faint and distant.

Notice two things you can **smell**.

Bring your awareness to the smells in the air, pleasant or unpleasant … like the smells of food from a nearby restaurant, fumes from the traffic on the street, or the perfume/cologne of someone standing close by.

Notice one thing you can **taste**.

Focus on what you taste right now. You don’t have to eat or drink anything, just notice the current taste in your mouth.

 1-Minute Mindfulness – Fond Memory

If you can, go somewhere quiet.

Close your eyes. Remember a time and place where you felt happy and at ease—maybe a vacation you had or a quiet evening in, snuggled up on the sofa. Call to mind the people who were with you. Think about what made this time special. Really visualise the scene and allow yourself to go there mentally. Hear the sounds, see the sights, smell the smells, and smile as you remember what a wonderful time this was.

Knowing that you can go back there anytime and that you will have more happy times like this in the future, go on with the rest of your day. Try to bring the happiness with you.

Everyday Mindfulness – Listening with Attention

Listening to others is something we all have to do. But are we always present for the person who's speaking, really listening to what they are saying? Try this simple practice whenever you are listening to someone talking. . .

Allow most of your attention to be on what the other person is saying and allow a little of your awareness to be on the sensation of your own breath. You should be conscious of your breath in the same way you might be conscious of a radio on low volume in the background. Listen to what the person is saying and how they are saying it. Be mindful of any reaction you might have to their tone or to the content of what they say. Sometimes these reactions can make us defensive when there is no need to be. Check that you are actually listening, not formulating your reply while the person is still speaking. All the while, be subtly alert to the feeling of your own breath.

One of the greatest gifts you can give to another person is the gift of your presence, your complete attention. Being fully present for them and what they are saying is a way of telling them: "I respect you and I want to hear what you have to say." Deep listening, listening intently, is a profound gift. The more you give it, the more you will get it back.

"Know how to listen and you will profit."

—*Plutarch*

Mindful Meditation – Movement

Take your meditation position. Spend a few moments making yourself comfortable.

Take a few deep breaths in through your nose. Release your breath through your nose slowly. Let your eyes close.

Bring your awareness to your body as a whole. Examine any feelings or sensations that may be present. Check your body. Are there any aches or pains? Now note any areas of tension—and note areas that are tension-free. Become familiar with all that is happening, all that is arising in your body, right at this moment. Try not to judge any feeling or any sensation you become aware of as “good” or “bad.” Just experience it. Don’t label it, question it, or get caught up in it. Let all feelings—all sensations—be as they are. Just *be*.

Gently now, continue to be aware of all feelings and sensations as they arise … and then fade away.

Now, decide to remain completely still, regardless of what sensations arise in your awareness. If you experience an itch, remain still. Resist the urge to scratch. Instead, examine the sensation of the itch. Note how it changes, becomes intense … then less intense. Notice how … eventually … it diminishes and is replaced by another sensation. Likewise, if you become aware of an ache, remain still. Just be curious about the sensation, about the ache. How does the ache change? Watch it as it fades.

Spend a few minutes sitting still. Sensations will arise in your body that will create the urge to move. Resist these urges—examine them instead.

Mindful movement is being aware of every part of any movement we make. This meditation is our practice for that. So, the next time we have an urge to move, we are not going to remain still but instead we will move, being mindful both of the movement and the cause of that movement.

As an example, suppose you are sitting cross-legged on your meditation cushion. Let's say you notice an ache in your right leg. Just as before, recognise the sensation. Examine it, become familiar with it. Don't react right away. Then make a conscious decision to move your leg. Notice every part of that movement … how do you shift your weight on the left side of your body? … what does that feel like? As you uncurl your leg, be aware of the movement in your hip, knee, and ankle. Notice how, when you stretch your leg out, the tension releases. As you bring your leg back to the cushion, focus your awareness on that movement. Finally, as you place your leg back into position, become aware of your body settling.

During the rest of your meditation, treat any other urges to move in this same way. If you become aware of a sound, make a conscious decision to move your head in the direction of the sound. Be aware of every part of the movement. Likewise, with an itch or any other sensation—just be aware.

When your meditation time is over, sit quietly for a moment or two. Congratulate yourself for your work in developing your mindfulness and awareness.

Try this…

As you go about your day, be aware of the movements you engage in repeatedly. When you reach out your hand to open a door, get up from your chair, answer the phone, or simply walk—bring your awareness to each part of your movement, every time you move.

"The best way to capture moments is to pay attention. This is how we cultivate mindfulness. Mindfulness means being awake. It means knowing what you are doing."

—Jon Kabat-Zinn

"Sit quietly. Be curious about what is present. Examine your sensations the way a child examines a crab in a rock pool—full of wonder and curiosity and without the slightest sense of judgement."

—Paddy Brosnan

1-Minute Mindfulness – The Other Room

Spend one minute imagining what is happening in the room behind, above, or below you.

If you're familiar with the room, picture the furniture and other contents. If you're not, imagine what might be in the room. Are there people in the room? What are they doing? What do they look like? Create an imaginary scenario in your mind. It doesn't have to make sense or be true to life in any way.

Mindfulness and Children

For those of us with children, I can think of no greater gift to give them than the practice of mindfulness. What could be more important for our children than having the tools to maintain their mental wellbeing and to foster good emotional and physical health?

The benefits of mindfulness for children are the same as they are for adults. The difference is that when you learn as a child to live mindfully, you have a greater chance of avoiding the stress and trauma most of us adults live with.

Here are some of the benefits of developing mindfulness in our children. Mindfulness…

- increases activity in the brain's frontal lobe, which is linked to improved attention, memory, and decision-making.
- increases children's ability to self-regulate their emotions—especially difficult emotions, such as fear and anger.
- increases self-awareness, social awareness, and self-confidence.

- improves children's empathy and awareness of others and helps them build positive relationships.

In the U.S., some schools have adopted a mindfulness programme called MindUP. In these schools the results have been astonishing. For example:

- Ninety percent of children improved their ability to get along with other children.
- Eighty percent of children were more optimistic and experienced enhanced self-regulation and self-management.
- Seventy-five percent of children improved their planning and organisational skills, had better impulse control, and reacted less.
- Incidents of bullying and absenteeism decreased.

Mindfulness in schools represents an important and incredibly beneficial change in how we teach our kids. However, as parents and guardians, we have a role to play as well.

We should encourage and foster mindfulness in our own children and in our own homes.

To my mind, generationally speaking, giving our kids a better life than we had is a great achievement.

Stress is contagious. Studies have shown that the greatest source of childhood and adolescent stress is not schoolwork, extracurricular activities, or peer pressure—it is parental stress—stress caused by our parents. We pass our stress down the line, literally. So, we have to start with ourselves, teaching by example, developing our own mindfulness, and living mindfully. Only when we have started this transformation in ourselves should we begin to teach our children. Remember, children are small, but they are not stupid. When we walk the walk (rather than just talking the talk), they will listen to us—and follow our lead.

"Too much love never spoils children. Children become spoiled when we substitute 'presents' for 'presence.'"

—*Anthony Witham*

Teaching the Kids

Just as for your own day-to-day activities, you can turn anything your child does into an opportunity to practice mindfulness. You simply need to guide them—normally, by prompting and asking questions.

Let's take brushing teeth as an example. Encourage your child to feel the weight of the toothbrush in their hand. As they squeeze out the toothpaste, ask, "Do you notice any smell or sound?" Continue to ask questions: "What does the paste feel like? Is it grainy or smooth?" "Can you feel the brush on your gums? What does that feel like?" You are not trying to get answers, you're asking them to consider these things internally as a way to focus their attention on the activity. You are teaching them to have their mind present, to be present with their body, in their environment.

When you go for a walk with your child, tell them: "Listen carefully. Can you tell you me when you hear a sound?" Ask them questions: "What is the sound? What does it remind you of?" Encourage your child to be curious, to examine their reaction to sounds they hear.

Set aside time each week to play with your child or children mindfully. Turn off tablets, TVs, games consoles—and put your own mobile away or on silent mode. Give your child your full attention during this time. If your mind wanders off to all the things you think you should be doing, that's fine. Gently bring it back. Each time your mind strays, use your child as an anchor to come back to. Encourage them to be fully present by showing them that you are.

I mentioned MindUP earlier. One of the core practices they use is what's referred to as a "brain break"—three or four minutes in which a child can breathe deeply and focus on their breath. This allows them a chance to quiet their mind and restore a sense of calm. This is a great exercise to use during homework or at other stressful times. The real power in this exercise lies in the fact that the child understands that it's okay to "take a moment" … that when they feel flustered, they won't be pressured further. Introduce this idea to your children; encourage them to ask for a "brain break" when they need it. If you see them getting stressed or frustrated, ask, "Do you need a brain break?"

Practice mindful breathing with your children every day. This will only take about five minutes. Use the biggest bed in the house and have everyone lie across the bed, with their head and feet on either side of the bed (not at either end). Squish everyone onto the bed—the closer together, the better. Nominate an adult to guide the meditation as follows:

"Everyone put one hand on their tummy and take a deep breath.

Close your eyes. Let your breath settle and breath normally.

Bring all your attention to your hand on your tummy.

Really focus on it. Can you feel it move when you breathe in and out?"

(Stay silent for a minute to let everyone, including you, feel this.)

"If your mind has wandered away from your hand and breath, just bring it back there."

(Allow another silent pause.)

"Now, see if you can feel the breathing movement of the person beside you."

(Again, allow time for this before you speak again.)

"Bring your attention back to your own breath and to the feeling of your tummy going up and down."

"Now, gently allow your eyes to open and don't move for a little while."

A great way to end this practice is with a big family hug!

"Twenty years from now you will be more disappointed by the things that you didn't do than by the ones you did do. So throw off the bowlines. Sail away from the safe harbor. Catch the trade winds in your sails. Explore. Dream. Discover."
—*Mark Twain*

Final Thoughts

We know from research that practicing mindfulness actually changes your body's biochemistry and rewires some of the neural pathways in your brain, resulting in changes in the structure of the brain itself. These changes have been found to be overwhelmingly beneficial.

I know from my own experience (and from the experience of other long-time mindfulness practitioners) that science is trying to measure a "felt" change, an experiential shift in how you live your life, because your life changes—for the better—when you live mindfully. You will be less prone to mood changes and more content and happier generally. Relationships with those you love flourish because you are more tolerant and caring. You have more time for yourself and the things you love to do because you become aware of all the unimportant, useless things you spend your time on and you cut them out.

You will suffer less from stress and anxiety, because your tendency to fall into the old, stale patterns of thought that cause you to worry and catastrophise will diminish. You will become aware of the negative stories and narratives that have been playing in the background constantly and let them go. This is incredibly liberating—your confidence and sense of self-worth will soar. Your self-care and your concern for the welfare of others will increase.

The world will become a less scary place (as will the people in it) and your sense that stuff is being "done to you" will decrease. You will realise, for example, that the person who just cut you off in traffic didn't pull out in front of you, they just pulled out; the queue isn't there because you are in a hurry, people are just queueing. You will respond to your thoughts and feelings instead of reacting to them. Moreover, because of your awareness you will be able to decide if you will respond at all. Your everyday, normal, mundane activities will become joyful and meaningful.

All this—and more—comes from twenty minutes of mindful meditation morning and evening and from bringing mindful awareness to the things you already do every day.

You are free to start at any time, why not now?

"Those who stand at the threshold of life always waiting for the right time to change are like the man who stands at the bank of a river waiting for the water to pass so he can cross on dry land."

—Joseph B. Wirthlin

"Plenty of people miss their share of happiness,
not because they never found it,
but because they didn't stop to enjoy it."
—*William Feather*

Acknowledgements

A word of thanks to everyone who helped put this Treasury together, Michael, Paul, Arlene and Susan. I am so grateful for all your help, advice and encouragement.

To my family, Faye, Tiernan & Odhrán – I can only do this work I love so much because of you and the support and love you give me. Thank you.

Very few come to understand the profound wonders of practicing mindfulness and living with awareness by themselves. I am no exception and I owe a huge debt of gratitude to my teachers. Without these beautiful human beings, I wouldn't know the happiness I do now.

Printed in Poland
by Amazon Fulfillment
Poland Sp. z o.o., Wrocław